Pretty Insanity

M. N. Creekmore

BookLeaf
Publishing

India | USA | UK

Made with ❤ on the BookLeaf Publishing Platform
www.bookleafpub.in
www.bookleafpub.com

Dedication

This collection is dedicated to Momma and Daddy,
To Tommy,
To Yaya and Jaja,
To my college professors, high school teachers, and
mentors who didn't have to read my rambling works but
did it anyways with a smile on their faces,
To all the writers I've ever met,
And to all my muses who made these poems possible.
(And of course to whoever invented the em-dash... I owe
you my life)

Preface

I was once told that every book has a story that led to it being created. For *Pretty Insanity*, mine comes from my love of anger. It doesn't mean what you think— I don't get a kick out of punching holes in walls or screaming at people, but I enjoy the fire of the deepest emotions, when there's just so much of it you can't do anything but sit there and say nothing. And then you turn water into wine: you write. But in all of it, the emotions are too thick and too intangible and too pure that you can say absolutely nothing, all while saying everything in the world through the silence of just existing.

That, and when the universe offers you cathartic release rambling and doing what you love, you just take it. You write the poem. You make the book.

The title *Pretty Insanity* comes from the fact that any one of these emotions which the following poems capture can be happening in someone's inner turmoil, yet they may still look just fine. They could look happy, content, even pretty, hence: pretty insanity. I'm sure you'll understand what I mean very soon.

Regardless, writing angry is normally called a bad thing. I've been told before that I write confusingly, that I write too flowery, that I write confidently, that I write engagingly, that I write very 'out there,' etc etc. But to me, I write angry. I love to write angry. I write my best when I'm angry. Anger is passion, and passion is writer-fuel— when passion is called 'love,' it's romantic and beautiful, so why should it be bad when that passion is called 'anger?'

Acknowledgements

Isn't this exciting? I wrote the book, and it looks like you're reading it! When I picked back up the writing of poetry some two years ago, it took me almost two hours to write one poem, perilously counting beats and singing rhymes, teaching myself what the word pentameter meant and fighting with metaphors and figures of speech to try and make what was grammatically, technically, and in a purely definitional sense 'poetry.' Then I discovered the joys of a good, chaotic free verse, and I don't think I'll ever look back.

I'd like to acknowledge some of the same people from in my dedication. Thank you, Momma and Daddy, for helping with emotional and financial support... sorry not sorry that most of my poems were based on angst. A thanks to you and Yaya and Jaja for proofreading my drafts and helping me choose which poems to submit, as well as providing endless streams of encouragement and incitation for more writing.

Thank you to my college professors who encouraged me when I divulged that I was working on this project alongside my very first full-time college classes. Particular thanks to Professor Bermudez, Professor Beasley, Dr. Unigwe, Profe Humphrey, and Dr. Gower. I won't name names, but one of these professors mistook me for a biology major once, and to that I say: thank goodness I'm not. It would never work out. Like really.

Special acknowledgements to the most prolific reader I've ever met, my brother Tommy. I really thought I was being discreet with half of my metaphors, but no one sees through you quite like a sibling. Hope I see a copy of this book on one of your best and tallest bookshelves soon.

I won't name everyone I've ever met, but thank you thank you thank you to all my friends who said they'd read a poem for me every now and then. You didn't know what you were getting into, but I appreciate you nonetheless. Thank you to my new college friends, sorority sisters, old friends, dance class friends, and class acquaintances for being all sorts of muses, proofreaders, and encouragers. Some of you asked if "I was okay" after reading some of these, and I promise I am. I just really like symbolism.

Thank you to all the support I've received from all my fellow teen and student authors and aspiring writers. You guys are the best. Special mention going out to I. R. Miller, one of the brightest-shining minds I've ever met. Glad to be joining you in the 'multiple books published' club.

Also, I still haven't figured out who invented the em-dash, but I thank Emily Dickinson for making it cool.

"Paper"

Paper essays, paper stars,
I loved you with a paper heart.
Folded golden stardust cluster,
Cut me with your modern art.

Origami nonchalantly, coat my hands in tar.
Click the scissors snapping apart
To dip them in your glitter, quitter,
To cut out my paper heart.

Crease me down my middle,
Riddle me— if it were quicker,
Would you hurt me if it hurt good?
Flickering like flame of liquor— only glimmer.

Hot glue sears, resin clear,
Punch a hole through my tissue chest
To spang me, hang me, beautifully,
In the gallery of fallacy, a virgin gest.

Paint a saint's face in every place
Not cracked or torn, wracked or shorn dispart,
On sticky, clicking pliers with wire
To cage this mage, my paper heart.

"Imagine What It's Like to Hate an Angel"

Imagine what it's like to hate an angel.
Imagine rage, mortal rage,
Picture the stones as they arc, flaming coal,
In your direction.
Smell the acrid reek of your flesh
As it scrapes off against the stake.
Feel your eyes burn slowly away
In the vicious bite of flame,
Burning sinfully white.
And now instead imagine
My robes black like richest chocolate,
Clashing with the broken shell
That enswathes her holy being.
White lily of the valley slowly suffocates
The fertile black soil below,
Still I am tried for treason
For hating an angel.

Maybe the celestial trumpet burst my eardrums,
Maybe the strings of the golden harp cut my fingers.
Imagine that,
Smothered slowly within an embrace,
Choking on a silken pillowcase

Like a corpse mistakenly laid to rest on their stomach.

My kind never graced the pages of the angel's gilded
books,
I only find myself in the curve of a pyre,
The gospelizing sinner hung on flint and cord,
Since a thousand eyes and a thousand wings
Never saw me,
Never reached me,
Despite how I never moved.
But I suppose she didn't move, either.

My lungs burn as I entreat this newspaper world
With the final chirps of a fallen chick,
Feathers ruffled and dirty with white mold rather than
molt,
Beak bent inward from never getting to sing.
Slowly, blindly, the mob blurs
Into fireflies on the wall.

Imagine dying for something you believe in
Yet not becoming a martyr.
Imagine becoming a cautionary tale
Only for existing,
Imagine what it's like to hate an angel.
My bones go exposed and char the same color they
condemned me for,

Like rotting teeth, gums peeled back—
You can never know what it's like to hate the angel.

"Stay—"

Stay.
Come on, it's just one word.
Stay—

I needed to wash the sheets, they were tied in knots
But my knees were bruised, they'd worn holes in all my
pants
I'd spent so long at your feet I forgot how to stand.
I should smile more, I should laugh more
At least pretend I'm having fun—
      Why did you go?
          Why did you go?
             Why did you go?
I said STAY just one word, one word, why did you go?
Was it because I hovered over you in your sleep
I had a knife in my hand, but it was made of glass
You turn me brittle, all my finger bones turned to dust
This poem isn't even about you, is it? It's about me
      Who am I?
Breathe, I'm breathing.
There's still air when you're not here.
But everything went dark, maybe that's why you're
gone,
I just can't see you

                                    Right?

               Cruel joke, awful prankster
You were always like this I don't know why I loved you
Did I love you?

                             breathe
You were there in all my phases, I'd wane and wax to fit
your hands
But the new moon was a trick, there's nothing left here
You lied — HA

               You're a liar.
                    You lied. (like liars do)
I asked you to stay and you disappeared
You're like a dog, a mutt, you can't even stay
I'm clawing my eyes out with the acrylics I bought you
There's skin beneath the nails, it's disgusting
scrub it out

                         this isn't my skin
               I want you out of me— GET OUT
Leave me alone
no stay why didn't you stay?

                                    Stay.
                         Stay.
Remember when we walked in the meadow
You picked a yellow carnation from the dirt
Half its petals were smashed, dilapidated, dying thing
You said it looked like me.
But you were wearing boots, I saw them, too big for your

feet

Covered in treads

Grass plastered to the bottom like blood.

   Damn you, your hair is red.

I want to go home, but I can't find you

             breathe

How do I go home when the door is off its hinges

There is no more plaster on the walls

Like skin it peeled away, revealing skeletons underneath.

We ran out of room in the closet

There's no more room in the closet.

…

Blood red gardenias,

Blood on the bathroom wall.

The stamens stammer out an alibi as you hammer the

petals till they

Bleed,

   Bleed,

      Bleed,

To remind you of the essence of me.

Like roadkill— you swerved

Lost a tire to the gods just to smash my whoopee-

cushion-ribcage.

Making me stay.

Stay— I can't move.

   …

    …

...

Stay. You'll stay. Say you won't leave. Don't leave me alone.

...

...

...

...stay?

"You're Beautiful"

Somewhere along the way I was convinced that blisters
meant strength.
Beads of precious nectar, crying scarlet teardrops in
silence—
Ruby encrusts my skin, gilding me in undeniable worth.
They proved that I could suffer, that I was trying.

Fushcia canvas stained from inside out,
The bandages of a soldier abandoned on the battlefield—
My body cannot be a temple, for I was the one sacrificed
On the stairs, drop-dead beautiful,
But this is just how we treat our favorite toys.

Wrap the pain in tulle and taffeta,
Bind the bruises in satin and the bones until they narrow
Stretch every muscle as thin as silken ribbon, then
tighter, tie in a knot,
Pull the sinew taut and bleed. You're beautiful.
Don't you feel it? You're beautiful.

Somewhere along the way the little girl in the teacup
tutu
Stopped chasing feathers across the stage, she cried 'help
me'.

They said—
Don't you feel it? You're beautiful.

"I Can Smell the Rain"

It's not raining outside.
Humans smell rain like blood in the waves,
Dorsal fins made of yellow plastic,
Raised high as we turn our faces to the ground,
Because we believe we can't fly
Because we believe the rain leads nowhere
Because since when does the map go backward?

A thousand droplets point straight down,
Polluted and misconstrued.
It's the motor oil leaking from the space machine,
The bile dribbling from an alien's lips,
The depressed tears of a cumulonimbus,
The wine of a naughty angel,
The spit of a chained-up god.
It's not raining tonight.

I'm lying in bed tonight, and I can smell the rain.
I smell myself too, soured like a lemon
Left out on the beach. Touch my skin,
Squelching with liquid that dribbles off the side of my
bed,
Into the carpet and my slippers beneath my bed,
Spilling through the holes of the laundry basket besdie

my bed.
I don't care, because I'm not in my bed.

The concrete kisses the backs of my arms and legs,
Little needles shape my skull.
The rains wash my flesh away,
The rains wash my sins away,
The rains wash me away,
To drain into an empty grave
At the end of the street.

I'm at the window and I smell the rain,
Cold glass pane cutting through my cheek
Until I cut through it,
Expression open to the sky.
I catch the farewells in my mouth, swallow,
And suddenly I can smell my insides,
How squishy I am inside,
Made of membranes like a chrysalis from the inside,
The hundred kinds of rain I have inside,
As if I swallowed every change that was supposed to
swallow me.

I never left my room last night,
I never left the bed,
I never sat by the window,
I never tasted the rains.

My skin is sheet, my hair cotton,
I open my mouth and threads spindle out, unraveling
slowly—
My sinuses clear.

I can smell the rain.

"Call Me Glitch"

- I'm the fault in the system (haha)
- "It's not me it's you" (HAHA)
You sent out mixed signαls
I transpired all the symbØls
Static, **static**, all I hear is **static**
Ha ha, Unwilling accomplic€ am I ! —ca11 me **Glitch**.

I'm a virus immune to antibiotics,
An addict with no need for psychotics.
Click — click — click   your mouse runs to me.

[hit r e l o a d...]

If I'm the €ntity disrupting the program
Who mαnifested my fau1ty diagram?
    Artificial intelligence, subhuman coding
inaccurαcy
Error, **Error**, all I see is **E r r o r**
    Is +hat all we were? Ha ha— then cal1 me Glitch.

    If   I'm   such a
©orruption,
    Binαry for a maniac
malfuncti0n,

Then all my words must m ak e n o sen s e t o y ou

Haha * Haha. (*it's funny, why aren't you laughing?*)
L∞k at you, inverted-backwards-sideways-frozen-
misplaced mess
10100011000— do you understand? Ha ha. **Call me
Glitch.**

"Blackberry Wine"

My blood runs thin, blackberry wine,
Twisting through my veiny vines.
My drunken stupor encases you
Like satisfaction encases the dead.
Broken bottle's what I am—
Once beautiful, now only damned.

Hunched over broken glass,
Surrounded by the working class,
My perilous petty paramnesia
Replaced your good sense with gluttony,
Expensive liquid in your flute,
Strangled from forbidden fruit.

Part my lips,
As it drips—
Cut me open with a spiral knife,
Broke the glass— spilled blackberry wine.
Turn your inner child to an alcoholic,
Uncorked my heart for sweet narcotic.

Dripping sorrows
That you borrowed,
Impulsive ruptures of blackberry wine

Entreat your wounds like razor blades.
How's it taste to swallow my pain?
All my sweetness makes for a bloody stain.

"Hurts Good"

It hurts whenever I walk, but it
                    Hurts good,
             Hurts good,
        Hurts good.
Bent to tie my shoe,
Vertebrae and muscles twist—
My body eats itself,
How did I end up like this?

(Fought an alley cat,
He didn't like that.)
Peeled an orange down to the spine,
Never learned how to draw in a straight line.
(Oh it hurts good,
      hurts good,
   hurts good.)

Lying in bed my bones curve like a funeral pyre,
The cathedral bell's crinoline,
The ribcage of God's least favorite creature,
The pages of an open book.
Cry out to the air if it'll listen, oh it
    Hurts good,
    Hurts good.

It's what I tell my preacher, tell the walls,
Tell my mother when she calls,
Tell the whole world if I knew the words to,
How I wobble when I walk,
Can't bend over,
Can't talk.
How long till I am
Something less than human?

Put together a puzzle last night but forgot one of the
pieces.
There's a hole in the middle now, I wonder if it hurts
good, hurts good.
Spent all night with tissue paper, smoothing all the
creases.
Tore a couple edges off, I wonder if it hurts good, hurts
good.
Watched a girl waiting on a street corner get stolen by
some sleazes.
Her nail broke on the car door, I wonder if it hurts good,
hurts good.

My pants don't fit,
Looking in the mirror hurts,
Oh it don't hurt good.
Straighten my body with my hands,
Like molding wet stuffing,

Oh it don't hurt good.

I just need to take the edge off,
Let my head hang between my legs, between my hands,
Take the edge off
     Take the edge off.
              How long till I'm something less than
human?
     (How long till I'm too human?)

Sat alone in my room last night, stressed about
All the things I have and haven't done.
All I could do was lay on my back
And wonder about the right tenses of all the words
In all the books on all the right topics
On all the shelves in all the right sections
Like an editor combing for one simple mistake in a
library full of classics.

Mental backflips are still real,
They don't tell you that in classes,
But I don't think they should.
              Oh hell,
           It comes in passes, and
        It hurts good,
     Hurts good,
Hurts good.

"Heart on my Shoulder"

It's strange, the
Things I do so readily
To get out of someone's way.
Slammed my shoulder into a shelf,
It looked kinda like a heart,
It looked kinda like you.
But it vanished slow—
Like you did not
It left scars—
Like you
Did.

"A Dark House"

There's something strange about this house
A whisper in the air, cold fingers up my spine
Color dissolves like smoke in the air
Yet the ash in the furnace becomes a shrine.

A specter looms over my shoulder
My mother, she calls out— "come back inside"
But from the window stretches her shadow
A memory, a breath long exhaled, already died.

In here a toddler learned to walk, to talk
A childhood faced sunrise and set within these walls
The laughter remains trapped in the floorboards
Juvenility still rots, the stench makes me a thrall.

Recollections grasp at my hair, equal in number.
I shave my head and its thoughts of olden times.
The childhood pictures above the mantle giggle,
And side by side with flattened candles, it all rhymes.

Down and down the stairs, the halls they multiply
Every mottled, mangled memory, how they distemper
Throw open the doors, the trees reach for me
As the darkness left behind screams "remember".

"Every (Bad) Thing You (N)ever Did"

Made tombstones out of shots and spirits,
Made ice cubes out of grain and ghosts,
Drowning deep in tears till the sirens sing my song,
Until the leaves merely rustle when you come around,
For you are something less than holy.

Maybe someday this will turn into a poem,
An epic ballad, a book, and a religion—
For it can never have a body. If it had a body
I could resuscitate it. If it had a body
I could keep it. If it had a body
I would have something to fight for.

And suddenly every bad thing you ever did became
Every bad thing you ever did,
When before now they were just things you did.

So God forbid I become an effigy
Of all the things you made me.
God forbid I show a crack in the wall,
That I reveal an essence of my damages.
God forbid I'm the sloppily covered-up scandal,
The glass foundations crumbling just after you laid them.

God forbid—
Why did you bring him into this?

You tore my pictures off the wall,
But did you realize you took yourself down, too?
Leaving a fist-sized, heart-sized hole in the wall—
Hypocrisy and heresy sound almost like our names.
You said I wasn't kind enough,
But was it kind when you tore out my ribs,
One by one, chewed on the ends,
And jammed them back in place
At the dinner table, in the dining room,
In front of Aphrodite and your parents—
Leaving a fist-sized, heart-sized hole in my chest.

I'm high on ibuprofen and Icarus's shoulders,
Every essence of us, I take with me,
Written in fire and old perfume.
I wedge the version of the you you used to be beneath
my fingernails
Trapped in gore, slowly melting as I near the horizon,
Melding into me. You are me.
You walk at my side forever this way—
You can be Adam, I can be Eve,
Maybe then this will be your wedding-bell dream.

I'm taking you all the places we don't go anymore

All while leaving you behind.
All while,
You paint your room bright green—
Black leaks through at the edges.
I hover at the baseboards, my muscles full of mildew
Coughing up moldy clouds as they relax,
Letting my drip drip down behind the pitch-thick walls.

One by one I pop my knuckles,
Pop my lips,
Pop the pimple at the place where my clavicle dips,
Slowly releasing the memories
One by one,
So they drop in a big brown suitcase at my feet.

Take it all the places we don't go anymore,
Doing all the bad things you ever did.
Take me all the places we don't go anymore,
Doing all the good things you never did.

"Love Like This"

It feels like passion, it feels like scarlet and burgundy
And all other shades of red. Color of blood,
Like fine wine in an intoxicated vermillion flood,
Losing control of yourself at the bottom,
Not knowing the bottom was in your bosom.
In my eyes a kaleidoscope of valentines, heart-shaped,
A jelly jar, glass busted, confines screwtaped,
Spinning, swallowing, saying to me
That is how you love. Like this.

Sitting at the top of the stairs,
Wondering how much it would hurt to fall,
Wondering if it would hurt at all.
Bright red hurricanes, feelings so big
My chest busts from the inside, so quick
That the whirlpool doesn't consume me,
The whirlpool is me, I am the sea,
Thought I figured it out, if anybody cares:
That is how you love. Like this.

If it doesn't hurt you aren't doing it right,
Love is big and powerful and feels a little like dying,
It's a little like crying without feeling,
Like feeling without crying, it's a little like

Eating ice cream in winter, a lightning strike
Coming from inside the body.
Feels a little bit godly.
I guess that's why they're all coming to fight—
That is how you love. Like this.

I don't want love like this,
But it's a crossword puzzle not designed to make sense.
Cross out the letters, they shove incense
Down my throat. But I don't want love like this.
Start to mumble 'if love goes like this,
I don't want any part of it,'
They say "oh what a tragedy, her throat's not slit"
But for once I make the bullet miss.
What's the point of love like this?

"Overcorrection"

All or nothing, cutting and running,
Tears turn into diamonds,
Nooses become rings.
I was always the exception—
Now I've become your overcorrection.

Swerve off the road,
Straight into the pits of hell.
Hand glued to my mouse, hitting 'reload'
But no matter how many times I spell
U and I, the code doesn't compute—
I've become a prostitute
For spare moments, second-hand minutes,
Laying in the flames,
Skin a patchwork of stains,
Left by a thousand fingerprints
And other configurations— transfigurations
From overcorrections,
Your beloved exception.

If you walk around the world far enough,
You'll retrace your steps.
You retraced straight back to me,
Straight. Back. It's funny.

Cherry blossoms, lilacs, bluebells, swaying
In a field of bent and broken rye,
A glistening ring around your eye
Tells you this isn't right—
Bend backward, swerve a 180,
Make an overcorrection.

Starve myself, then gorge afterward,
As if I could heal a wound by filling it with knives.
Pain doesn't go away
By putting love on top—
I don't know what it's like to die,
I don't know who lined my dermis with steel,
But it means I don't bounce back.
There is no rebound,
There is no overcorrection.

All or nothing, cutting and running,
Memories turn to sins,
Passion becomes dangerous.
I was always the exception—
But I won't be your overcorrection.

"Margaret"

I never met a Margaret,
I never learned to dance.
Piqué pretty pirouettes,
Call me Peggy or Maggie or Margarita, but
I never met a Margaret,
I never learned to duel.

Beautiful baby, lets put a tutu on you,
Another cog in the machine,
Oh they're coming for you
Now— nobody can hear you scream.
Mercutio plagues a curse on every room,
A masquerade ball
Wearing silks, coming undone, unglued,
Blow a fuse, sticking a hairpin
Into the electrical socket by the bar(re),
Slowly the syllables keep coming, counting,
One-two-three,
Mar-gar-et.

Sell me like a piece of meat,
A single rose,
A shooting star.
Princes catch my waist,

Mercutio claims my blood for his own,
Lord and Lady lounge in the theater,
Bum bum dun da.
Wishing they'd gone to see a different show.
Bum bum dun da daaa.

Can't escape the acts, 1-2-3-
Acting, scenery, soliloquy, iambic tragedy,
I never learned pentameter,
Jump off the Eiffel Tower
With my arms full of ribbons, engagement rings
On every finger.
Perhaps there are roses left in Paris.

Seventh position, break my neck, soubresaut,
Feet so straight, an eternal sauté,
Clasping hands, moving hands, holding hands,
And my face then seems to say
"Catch me, catch me, Romeo."

My name's not Rosaline or Juliet,
But my name could be Margaret,
One-two-three
      One-two-three
            One-two-three.
My name could be Margaret,
Maybe I'm just Rosaline.

Juliet never has to lift herself,
While I'm hand-in-hand with a faceless Mab.
I've never met a Margaret.

"An Evening Spent Looking in the Mirror"

I am the vein glimmering blue across the top of the shin. And the Universe— a teenage girl endlessly picking her skin.

"Big"

You like music. You like your clunky black headphones,
With the cord as long as your arm.
Plug it in like an artificial artery
To the hand-me-down brick from your mom.
Scroll the songs— J-Lo and Prince,
Listen to the beat as it drones,
Say 'what's the harm,'
Because everybody likes music.

Your 'friends' like music. Wireless speakers,
They hold their organs outside of their chests,
Like corpses, like angels, like masochistic sickness.
Pearly pink speaker in the hands of a goddess,
Call God and a preacher, here comes the raptures,
She smiles at you. Everyone likes music.

You gather with everybody else when the pearly pink
speaker comes out.
It's pretty, it's perfect—just an adject
Of preppy, of popstar, of in-style and on-trend,
You've never heard this music before.
Pretty, perfect, preppy, popstar,
You're not any of these things.
You're

Just
Big.

They call you big. Everybody calls you big.
Big, behind, bloated, bothersome,
But everybody likes music.

You memorize the name of a pretty, perfect, preppy
popstar,
She's blonde she beautiful she's rich,
You leave your headphones at home.
Your heart slowly stops beating.
You start to feel a little monochrome,
Because just last night you stopped eating.

What did they call you?
Big. Turn up the volume— *big.*
Rhymes with pig.
You blast the popstars on replay, an IV drip
Of brand-new blood. Bite your lip,
Because if you're like them on the inside,
Nobody even sees the outside.
Lie back in the hospital bed,
Your face turning red,
From crying on the inside
Because only babies cry on the outside.

You get invited to birthday parties,
Because all the moms of your 'friends'
Want you around. They think that
Their daughters will stop getting piercings, boyfriends,
push-up bras, dress codes
If they just hang out with you.
It's all so big.
They did, in fact, turn off those roads
Just to whisper about you.
Big, big, big huddles around your head.

Your 'friend' offered you some chocolate at her birthday
party,
Who knew you were supposed to say no and be snarky.
They laughed while you ate. Said 'big'—
Said 'big, big, big'—
You decided you'd never eat chocolate again.
Because the ideal girl can sustain
The best when she's wonderfully sick
And unhappy girls are the sickest.
You suggested music. Everybody likes music.

The pearly pink speaker shines brighter than you.
It beats and it drones, vibrates with tones,
The pearly pink speaker is more loved than you.
You ask for the pretty, perfect, preppy popstar.
They laugh.

They all laugh.

Your parents are angry with you,
Watching, sighing, stealing from you.
You cover the sharpie on your flesh, marking everything
You'd like to delete.
And even as the years go by,
You still cry sometimes when you eat.
Your friends say you're sick.
You just turn up the music.

Scream to the world that you know that you're sick,
Covering your parents ears,
But drown out the echo when it comes back around,
Because it sounds like your 'friends,'
It sounds like the speaker activating,
It sounds like laughter, and it blends
Into a chorus crying:
You're
Just
Big.

"Like"

I like burnt red lipstick
I like talking to my mom.
I like eating popcorn
And I don't like being wrong.
I like pretty earrings,
I like glitter on the floor.
I like how I'm okay with
How we don't talk anymore.

Stupid music with my father,
Stupid games inside my head.
I like how part of me someplace inside
Is lying very dead.
I really like my sister
Only because she doesn't exist,
I like however that she still has veins
Lining inside her milky wrists.

I like pretending the mirror's a picture,
Not some chick on Facetime.
I like the clanky sound my jewelry makes
When I'm searching for a rhyme.
I like how I lie to myself
With a wreath of roses around my neck,

I like how the thorns feel
Against my ethereal itch, my ghostly wreck.

I like reading with my grandma
I like eating chocolate chips
I like seeing girls with bigger thighs
And wider female hips.
I like gummy worms
And gummy bears
I like people wearing button ups
And fun underwear.

I like driving long roads alone,
I like candy that tastes like shit.
I like getting paint everywhere,
But not eating any of it.
I like pretty people
With butterflies in their eyes,
I like how it flutters now and then,
When they smile, when they lie.

I like pink hair
And juicy watermelon.
I like tiny clay figures
And releasing muscle tension.
I like the melodic sound
That windchimes make

Even when they're on the ground—
I even like my memories, as warped as the moon.

"Lollipop"

The priest looked upon me,
Broken on the alley floor,
Trod upon by gypsies and hipsters
Cracked along the edges—
Shards, merely shards,
Too sharp for a rich woman's throat
And he said "God has walked here"
In regard to the footprint on my forehead.

I didn't know God wore Nikes—
I didn't know Nike was God, was breaking me.
He kicked aside my stem and root,
In case it mussed the hem of his robe;
Called me stained glass,
Said I'd look good in bars of lead
Said "God would love me better that way"
As if God didn't make me a lollipop.

"The World Ended"

And suddenly,
>> The world ended.

The blink of an onyx eye in the distance
Like a star going out—
Somebody's sun on somebody's planet
Leaving a colony of squatters to suffocate
And turn over cold in their beds.
They're shivering, I watch them quivering
While I wrap a coat around my shoulders,
Letting myself sit.

The cold air shocks their lungs
While I breathe easy, the weight off my chest,
Cutting the cord to my adoptive mother,
Instead of sitting in the slackening horizon of somebody
else's fate.
Watch it sag like the lips of a godless king,
Like an old front porch,
That somebody didn't keep up over the years—
No, instead they sat. They sit.
I let them sit.

In the blink of an onyx eye I see

All the reflections in the darkness,
Like when my phone dies just before from my face
Leaving the image of my face outlined for once in white.
I see peace kneeling at the steeple of my ribcage,
Before the throbbing muscle that
believed in me
And I let myself sit.

"Pretty in my Brain"

Gotten to the point I'm not pretty when I'm real.
I'm not pretty when I look down,
I'm not pretty when I turn around,
Gotten to the point where pretty isn't real.
So I
Chopped off my face and everything on it
Locked it in a box,
They're saying I lost it
But I know right where it went.

I remember when midnight was far away
I remember when I'd never heard the bells before
Much less twelve times
Ringing, dinging through my brain
Until it splinters, dissolves through my bloodstream—
My thoughts are all of me.

Discipline, strike my shin,
Where the veins run across it.
Spill my blood, spill my thoughts,
Watch them pool, watch them pour,
I paint pictures on the floor.
My mirror's red—
I see myself.

Call it gore,
Call it obedience,
No one asked for my two cents.
But they asked for more.

I can't see the knife well enough to clean it,
I can't feel it either— that's no rag, is that my face?
I still know it's sharp.
You forgot about that.

The beauty's in my brain,
Counting shells as they strike the clock face— my face—
A war to release the pretty parts of me,
Violence to show them to you.
You scrub it from the grout and tile,
Would you wipe my makeup away, too?
No.
No, you wouldn't.

"How to Go Insane"

1. Try to make hot chocolate with water. Realize you've
just made hot brown water. Cry.

2. Try to lick the spoon— it burns. It was supposed to
kiss you, but it bit,
Lay down and cry, cry, cry.

3. Break the mug, throw the spoon, scream and spit,
Sit and stare at the wall a minute,
Count the imperfections along the plaster along-shelf,
Turn your finger back at yourself.

4. Think of every sentence your mother ever said,
Wonder what she said when you were something worse
than dead.
Return to your lover, in shards on the floor,
Realize that the spoon survived.

5. Hold the spoon in your hands like a baby bird,
It burns, but kinder now, splinters of glass
Digging into the soles of your feet. The hot brown water
Will probably grow mold like corroded brass,
But you clutch the spoon, and on every third word
You find yourself stuttering what you never heard.

6. Realize you're a pretentious bitch.
Throw the spoon away— even a small burn hurts
eventually.

7. You've made hot chocolate a thousand times. Have
you ever used water before?
Normally it's milk. Or cream. Or half and half. You can't
remember.
Dump the contents of cream packets into the depths,
Stir with your hands, feel it burn, then deplore
That your hot brown water spilt all over the floor—
You're stirring nothing, you're burning yourself.

8. Try to cry, realize you can't,
Want to cry even badly-er,
Realize it doesn't matter what you want.

9. Do you remember what it's like to cry?

10. Something in you breaks as you notice
No one else is in the room with you.
You're alone in there. All your friends
Dove beneath the surface,
So I guess they weren't your friends,
And there's nothing you can do
About that.

11. Put the hot chocolate mix away. It looks, now,
Like the dirt piled up next to the casket.
Try to be nice to yourself, try the things
Your therapist told you to do. Forget how.

12. Watch everything go up in flames.
Forget if they loved you.

13. Feel freed.

14. Ask yourself where all the time went to.
Ask yourself what happened to all the people
Who swore they'd never leave you.

15. Write a poem about all these things that make you
feel ill—
Know that you'd be rotting into the bed straps of a
mental asylum
If you'd been born enough decades ago.

15.5 Think of who would have been most likely to
commit you
To a cell.

16. Think about your sweet sixteen.
You don't actually remember it.

Don't you miss before pre-teens?

17. Became sane amidst the torture.

18. See if you were right about your choice in number
fifteen and a half,
Give up on crying and laugh.
Sit down and laugh, laugh, laugh.

19. Try to make hot chocolate with water. Realize you've
just made hot brown water.
Turn to heaven or hell, doesn't matter which one,
And ask for the name of their daughter.
Whatever they say, it doesn't matter,
All that matters is the fact that
Nothing will ever come after nineteen.